THE POWER
BRIGHT
AND SHINING

THE POWER
BRIGHT
AND SHINING

GREATEST HITS, VOL. I

GREATEST HITS, VOL. II

CHILDREN'S SONG BOOK

CLASSICAL MUSIC

BALLET

AMERICANA, R.F.D.

POINT/COUNTERPOINT

SEVEN ELIZABETHAN DANCES

THE MINOTAUR (MAN TO
   HIMSELF)

VOLGA SONG

FULL CIRCLE

THE PLAINS OF MY COUNTRY

DANCE YOUR ASS OFF

DIVERTIMENTO FROM THE
   BLACK EAGLE

OPERA AND CHORAL WORKS

THE BLACK EAGLE

TWELVE NEW CHRISTMAS
   CAROLS

CONCERTOS

FOR PIANO & ORCHESTRA

FOR CELLO & ORCHESTRA

FOR ORCHESTRA & VOICE

FOR GUITAR & ORCHESTRA

#2 FOR PIANO & ORCHESTRA

FOR FOUR HARPSICHORDS

SYMPHONIES & SYMPHONIC
   SUITES

SYMPHONY #1

SYMPHONY #2

BALLAD OF DISTANCES

THE CITY

SYMPHONY #3

Rod McKuen

THE POWER
BRIGHT
AND SHINING

Images of My Country

CHEVAL BOOKS
SIMON AND SCHUSTER
NEW YORK

COPYRIGHT © 1980 BY ROD MC KUEN AND MONTCALM PRODUCTIONS, INC. INTER-
NATIONAL COPYRIGHT SECURED. ALL RIGHTS RESERVED. PUBLISHED BY SIMON AND
SCHUSTER, A DIVISION OF GULF & WESTERN CORPORATION. SIMON & SCHUSTER BUILD-
ING, ROCKEFELLER CENTER, 1230 AVENUE OF THE AMERICAS, NEW YORK, NEW YORK
10020. SIMON AND SCHUSTER AND COLOPHON ARE TRADEMARKS OF SIMON & SCHUSTER.

DESIGNED BY EVE METZ
MANUFACTURED IN THE UNITED STATES OF AMERICA
1 2 3 4 5 6 7 8 9 10
LIBRARY OF CONGRESS CATALOGING IN PUBLICATION DATA
MC KUEN, ROD.
THE POWER BRIGHT AND SHINING.
"CHEVAL BOOKS."
1. UNITED STATES—POETRY.   I. TITLE.
PS3525.A264P6   811'.54   80-15264

ISBN 0-671-41392-9
ISBN 0-671-41393-7 (DELUXE ED.)

The poem "The City" is adapted from the musical work *The City*, © 1973 by
Rod McKuen and Stanyan Music.

The poems "Position" and "Prejudice," © 1973 by Rod McKuen and Montcalm
Productions, appeared in *Woman's Day* and in the book *Celebrations of the Heart*.

The poem "Parading the Colors" is a revised version of "Colors of the Flag," ©
1976 by Rod McKuen and Montcalm Productions. "Colors of the Flag" appeared in
the bicentennial issue of *Family Weekly*.

The poem "To the Last Man Carrying the Last Gun" appeared in the book
Beyond the Boardwalk, © 1975 by Rod McKuen and Montcalm Productions.

*Further information may be obtained by contacting the Cheval/Stanyan Company,
8440 Santa Monica Boulevard, Los Angeles, California 90069*

TO "THE GOOD GRAY POET"
Living Inside Every American

CONTENTS

9

AUTHOR'S NOTE

I refuse to apologize for my country. Though I can smell corruption and there is some, in August I can smell the wheat and it is stronger. Our gains in this the most unusual of all countries still outnumber by leaps our losses.

Because we are told the country is sick, even by a man elected to take charge, does not mean we are . . . though with enough repetition the rumor takes on proportions and the guise of fact. But as Americans we must speak with one voice and say NO. No to ever bigger government. No to violence and mischiefmakers. No to those we gave a nod to only yesterday who by now have proven their inadequacy, inability, and lack of responsibility as leaders of this nation.

The country has some headaches, but a probe for cancer would find the lumps benign. This nation has no wound so deep that it cannot be covered by a single strip of gauze, wrapped round and round. And what if the wounded have the power of healing too? I believe all people here are so empowered. The rhyme is in the rowing of the boat—straight ahead, not veering, except to take on passengers. Steady hands that circle sturdy paddles propelling us forever forward.

I am alarmed at any arm not getting on with it, lifting its own weight or writing words so fast they scorch the paper.

I admit I'm dangerous. Defile my country with ill attention or an ax and you slander me. I am my country as I am myself. Though I may travel down a thousand shores and wave at many thousand more, I intend to live and die on this my own ground.

A nation great? The best. A power bright and shining? Beyond—far beyond the edges or circumference of the Earth.

Please do not misunderstand. I will complain as long as wrongs need righting. But apologize? I am too busy trying to give back my share to offer an apology of any kind for a country that doesn't need one.

Rod McKuen
February 1980

. . . the genius of the United States is not best or most in its ambassadors or authors or colleges or churches or parlors, not even in its newspapers or inventors . . . but always most in the common people.

—Walt Whitman
from the introduction to the original edition
of *Leaves of Grass*, published in 1855

THE POWER BRIGHT AND SHINING

OUT OF
THE DARKNESS

America is an idea. Born out of need, nurtured into something from nothing—but everything; the hands and headaches and hearts of God's great handfuls needing freedom. Despite the years that pass or are passing, the country is still in its first days. Youth affords everything and the young see daylight first.

AMERICAN LANGUAGE

American names go rolling off the tongue
like rivers of rain down silver sidings
Chippewa and Idaho, Connecticut and Maine,
California, Arkansas, Georgia and Seattle.

Like stairs climbed often they lead us upward,
                              forward, ever onward
Wisconsin, Savannah, Corpus Christi, <u>Kansas City.</u>
Not just great states and awesome cities
but nicknames, too, ring out—
Yankee, Buckeye, Hoosier, and High Pockets.
More color finds its way into our speech
than all the Arizona sunsets.
Wolverine and Wahoo, Beaver Dam and Boulder Dam.

Sometimes it seems as though collectors
in Salvation Army uniforms
                      complete with tambourines
hiked across the land
picking this word up and dropping that
until a cornucopia of thoughts became so full
it overflowed and spit out sentences
that started an evolutionary dictionary.

Consider the rivers.
Mississippi, Allegheny, and the River Platt.
The lakes like Erie, Huron and Mead
the waters that somersault over Niagara.
Consider the names of American tribes
the true pioneers who founded this land
Chattahoochee, Arapaho, Navajo, Crow,
Comanche, Chickasaw, Chapolapec, Sioux.

And Spain by way of Mexico
charged in and changed the old vocabularies
from squared-off English to American.
Caliente comes to mind and Amarillo
and all the names derived from saints—
San Angelo and San Francisco, Santa Barbara
                              and St. Pete.

Some settlers brought their own names
                    out of Europe
contributing and distributing
a spate of words so spacious
that to list them would be just to make a list.
Pride from mother countries came
and with them Little Italy,
Chinatown, New Orleans, and New England.
The slang that ambled out of Africa—
honed in Harlem, washed in Watts—
now stretches coast to crowded coast
like some new copper pipeline.

But the continent itself let go of words
that ring like sleighbells
                    clang like cymbals
                              beat like drumming
and blast the ear like God's own trumpets.

Few states within the States
do not have resting places
that when said aloud
                    provoke a conversation.
Cathedral Gorge in Utah, California's Capistrano,
The Poconos, Tuckahoe, and Tonawanda.
Rivers, tribes and mountain peaks
                         cities and the plains
meet and mix in mad profusion
till who's to say—not history books—
which came first, the tribe or river
the tribesman called his home.

It is a rich and ruddy language
full of sweet and salty talk,
one that should be held aloft as badge and banner.
It even sounds good mispronounced.

And where but in America
                    could weaponry contribute?
Bazooka, Tommy, the Gatling gun
                         and Sunday Musket.

As we survey the now no longer
                    distant stars
and count the new heads
still on their way
to seek out freedom here,
so many words of wonder brush the ear
that dictionaries in the making
            die on publication date.

Every day some new word stops,
looks around, then settles in the land.
A poet, among other things, should help protect
                    his country's language.
Even as he versifies, he adds,
                subtracts, and multiplies.
This poem, then, inspired by the land
the love and luck of living here
observing and conserving words
is by necessity and not neglect
                to be continued.

What I've left out this time 'round
I'll pick up another—and another
until the time when speech
with new words being added
is drawn and done and ending.

But since a language has no ends
                              and no beginnings
I'll be long in dust before it's over.

I charge new bards to take up
these remarks and this go-round
add, amplify, and explain away
the talk they hear that no book
                    nor The Daily News
picks up and uses.

And for every metaphor she adds
and for every adjective he chooses
drops an older one that's worn
or wasn't right enough to find
its place upon the tongue
the first time out.

OUT OF THE DARKNESS

Out of oppression into freedom.
Out of constraint into expansion.
Out of the reading of history
into the making of history.
Out of iron shackles into producing iron.
Out of the man at the foot of the thinker
emerges the thinker himself.
Out of the bonds of forced religion
into the makings of new religions.
Out of the land cordoned off by the King
into the free and open country.
Out of weakness confirmed by labor
into strength produced by labor.
Out of the darkness into light.

Out of the rigid handed-down law
into the making of laws that are workable.
Out of the woods that has no clearing
into the clearing of woods.
Out from under the ruling class
into the class that rules itself.
Out of generations of sorrow
into generations of joy.
Out of poverty into pride.
Out of slavery into ownership.
Out of the scourge of being victim
into the role of benevolent victor.
Out of the galley and into the gallery.
Out of the twilight, free in the midnight.

Out of the mothers who mourned for their sons
now come the women at morning's first sunlight.
Out of the fathers who died in the struggle
now come the struggling founding fathers.
Out of the lands where sons played on cobblestones
into the country where sons turn the earth.
Out of the breath of daughters who died
in the bed of the serf, at the hand of pestilence,
a new generation of daughters with pride.
Out of the neighborhood bent with hunger
onto the block with belly full.
Out of the dungeon into the daylight.
Out of the need to gorge, into the need to give.
Out of the mineshaft into the air.

Away from the path that persecutes patriots
onto the highway that patriots paved.
Free from restraints of knowing yourself
finding how much of yourself you can know.
Released from the shackles of building for others
learning the craft of building for you.
No more apples from the barrel's black bottom
only the fruit from the green apple tree.
The demons dreamed up by the weak and afraid
give way to the dreamer controlling his dream
setting in motion his wide-awake visions
molding the axle to turn every wheel.
Out of the way of the sword and the shield.
Out of the well and into the water.

So came the foreigner, soon to be friend.
So came the misused, soon to be unified.
So came the lovers to beget generations.
So came the ill, soon to be well.
So came the indolent, to work for themselves.
So came the convicts, soon unchained.
So came the pilgrims, soon to be pioneers.
So came the builders, to carve a new country.
So came the hungry, to fill up their bellies.
So came the ignorant, soon to be learning.
So came the believer, allowed his beliefs.
So came the thinkers, to study in freedom.
So came the leaderless, soon to be leaders.
So came the few, soon to be many.

Speeches delivered, started the history.
Songs were passed round, till they were anthems.
Spread was the word that became fair law.
Swingers of axes cleared out the underbrush.
Soil was turned over for field and for garden.
Sown were seeds, healthily harvested.
Smiles were fence posts before there were fences.
Sailors sailed in on tides of tomorrow.
Sorrow was turned into joy by the neighbor.
Silence was broken by the splitting of rails.
Still in its infancy the nation was growing.
Soon men of principle drafted a paper,
providing the land with it's first constitution,
stamped by the seal of brotherhood's hands.

And pilgrim's pride and father's pride
pride of the mother made the child proud.
More than the word was the will and wonder
as each set of eyes set a goal for itself.
As each one prayed to his own God privately,
man and his family stretched out and grew.
He dug up the valleys and planted the corn,
sliced off the mountaintops and dug out the coal,
loaded the flatcars that rolled to the cities
and dammed up the waterways till there was power,
stretched out the cable and strung up the lights.
Pride was the tool that powered our progress,
need the dividing point sectioning land.
Love the explainer, settling arguments.

This land of giants was ground out of greatness,
and built on a firmer foundation of rock.
Each pioneer's progress and each of his setbacks,
each war and peace and each war again,
people not born, those knocked down by death
those who came here to find life and living
those whom we captured and those we set free,
those who died while defending the nation
and those *we* defended who couldn't be saved.
All of us still in Whitman's old cradle
endlessly rocking, endlessly rocking
still in the morning of life as we know it,
still looking up to the forehead of freedom
above and beyond our forefather's knee.

This is the country, this the place
all men of wisdom, worry and want
look to for freedom and freedom they see.

PARADING
THE COLORS

He or she who hasn't stumbled in the public garrisons and been picked up by strangers or a friend still trembles on the edge of life awaiting entrance. What's right with America are those who go on righting our wrongs.

ANTHEM

A handshake
is my pledge of allegiance.
My anthem
is my brother's shoulder.
My flag is the smile
on every face
stopping long enough
to return my own.
We've come down the road
               a long way
but there are miles
as yet unwalked
as yet unpaved.

FACES OF FREEDOM

A leader is a man or woman
                demanding of respect,
like a father or a God
not someone who will send his legion
to slip behind the borders of another nation
pocketing the payload for the hit man.

We investigate the arsonist
who sets the city block ablaze,
but who among us brings to trial
the men who sent our children
                off to all the Asias
until the nation bored with body bags
unloaded on the T.V. screen each night
switched channels to another rerun
                        of *Dobie Gillis?*
Who gave us righteousness enough
to burn five thousand years
of someone else's culture
        to the ground?

South of this America another lies
and yet we often treat our other half
as though she were a stranger
or we milk her till she's almost dry
as if she were a cow we pastured
and then branded with the iron
                              of total ownership.
Amazed, aroused, antagonized
we watch as she becomes a stranger.
Didn't we buy and pay for her, some ask.
How can any satellite of ours
                    have ideas of her own?
Long ago the man who keeps the ledger
                              in the Pentagon
lost count of all the fold-up beds
our agents slither under
in the guise of national security.

Some of us have started wondering
if this country's primary business
has not become the business of
                    other countries' business.

At first we bartered for the black man,
then made him row his boat
to what for him would be unfriendly shores.
Enslaved for one whole century
his complete emancipation still
remains on fading paper.
Though freedom pounds his heart
                              to early death
and beats within his mind
it has not started ringing in his ears.
The grim reality, one hundred years ago
that made him choose
                his master's surname
                      for his own
                          hangs on.
And now the world is meddling in his fatherland,
deciding as we did with our own native Indians
                    (make that Americans)
which piece of land or resource
on that black-green continent
will benefit which other country most.

Indian.
Indian chief.
Indian squaw.
Indian brave.
Indian reservation.
American Indian Ghetto.

Is the native son and daughter
worth a word or mention?
They'll soon be gone, extinct, deceased.
Or looked upon with awe
                    just like the buffalo
                        that used to feed
                            their nation.
The minerals in reserve
upon their meager reservations
            are in reserve for us.
I doubt an act of congress
                will be needed
to assure our taking over of the deed
or the doing of the deed itself—
mid-east crisis . . . all of that you know.

Shame? Too weak a word,
but there is no other.

Freed from England's bondage
we tried to buy her for our own
but she's as proud as any one of us.
The loans we made she repays with interest.

We can no longer bribe great nations
or their satellites to be our friends.
Do the histories of civilizations
                    others' and our own
teach us nothing?
Friendship is a hand extended
                not a checkbook
or a never-ending line of credit.

Because we're strong
and will grow stronger if we try
we should always offer help and hope
to our near and far-off friends,
but I.O.U.'s that lead our comrades
into attitudes and postures
that go against their cause and country
should cease to be repayment on demand.

What happened?
Did the government bust its britches
while the populace was busy
at leisure in our leisure suits?
Did the monitor leave the room?
What time was it? What year?
What moment did we look away
trusting the elected without question,
electing to let others other than ourselves
run the country like an octopus,
its tentacles so far-reaching
they stretched beyond our borders
and off across the length and width
                of this wide planet.

The road back's never easy,
but asphalt badly laid must be repaired.
Government must be handed back
                into the people's hands.
Too much needs doing in our yard
                sea to shining sea.

There has been no time
within our history or our history books
when patriots were not essential,
not one hundred years ago
                    tomorrow or today.
Keep your thumb upon the country
                    to monitor its pulse,
do not pass a mirror
without looking at yourself—
remember that *you* are the country.

The responsibility to keep the nation
for ourselves and for our sons and daughters
cannot be abrogated or passed over
to this official or to that bureaucrat.
To do so is to give the hard-earned land away.

We must be gardeners again
to keep the country growing.
Too many seedlings have been sacrificed,
too many trees have gone untrimmed,
too many hedges stay untended.
The farmer, not the fighter, has the tools.

Where just cause for fighting does exist
we'd better learn once more to battle in the open.

Democracy is delicate.
Beware the covert action
lest it become a habit
too instilled within ourselves
                        to be undone.
Pay attention to detail,
or inattention getting in
will weaken what we term *the main*.

Freedom is the forehead of the morning.
We risk the darkness if we fail to monitor
each law enacted and tacked on
to already bulging constitutions.

Stop apologizing for America.
More and more the ill that some men do
is hung out on the line
           for all mankind to see.

There will always be the negatives
who try to pull the positives down
               to their side.
Your job is to resist in all ways
               any way you can.
You will find that kindness
to your country and yourself
comes easily and is done with ease.
To hurt something you love is difficult
and takes no imagination.

QUESTIONS NEVER ANSWERED

Why is it
when a city stumbles
from lack of government support,
mismanagement or whatever
the first thing cut in that week's budget
is aid to schools and schools themselves?
Teachers are the first
to reach the unemployment line
         and the last to leave it.
Have we forgotten, or doesn't anyone believe
that in a country of green forests,
land aplenty, bullion in the bank,
        buildings tall and beautiful
the only asset that this nation—
any nation seeking freedom really has
           is its children.
How dare the city fathers in a conclave
        at the mayor's bidding
prune the country's future to a single stem
before it's had a chance to grow and bloom
           and blossom.

Free enterprise,
the path of those with talent
to make something out of nothing
                            built the highways,
and the trucks to travel down them—
hooked the light switch to the bulb
and made the back room laboratory
where the bulb was built.
Yet if an Edison came through the crowd today
what doorways would be open to him?
How would he fare and would he fare?
Surely there are Mozarts in the crowd,
                            Einsteins and Nightingales too
but bureaucracy is busy with its building blocks,
making mazes thick as Mondays,
trapping talent in its tracks,
retarding minds before each channel, each canal,
has had the chance to let a stream of thought
                            flow through it.

Some of us had hoped
that once a man walked on the moon
we'd go on reaching out to other stars.
Who would have dreamed that *space*
would become but one more catchword
                    coined by cults pursuing *self*?
And real space, expansive as it is,
would end up cluttered with the carcasses
of dynamos that dropped off from the mother ships
                    that went exploring?
This globe turns on and on
and isn't ready for discarding
but shouldn't we still plow past planets
                    we already know
toward the new adventure?
Must curiosity be sacrificed to sloth
or should our need to know the unknown
be saved and savored for collapsing telescopes
that reach no further than our neighbor's bedroom.

Some of us don't give a damn what people do in bed
unless we happen to be in on the act
                    and one of them.

Man is energy.
The only energy our country has is Man.
The lineman strings the wires till they sizzle.
The scissors of the scientist slice the atom.
The miner finds the coal and carries it
from corridor to corridor to the mineshaft opening.
Since government must have a hand in everything,
the dealer in some alien land
and not the speculator here at home
                    throws deciding dice for oil.
We are the only country held at ransom
by other nations left alone to work
and find their fortunes by filling up
                        our tanks and lamps
while we have fuel aplenty on this continent,
                    if not within these borders.

Again the government has interfered—
            we're told they're talking.
Expect decisions any moment now.
Why is it other governments less rich in resource
                            than our own
are halfway home in solving power problems?
Perhaps they know that Man is energy,
the only energy a country has is Man.

I'll say this for television;
I own one and I watch it often.
It brings in little bits of information
not found in any history book.
Not long ago I watched a young man questioning
a panel of programmed presidential hopefuls—
out of work he volunteered
            that there were jobs available
but all of them paid less
than his untaxed and probably unearned
                        unemployment checks.
Why work when those who do
pay handsomely for me to play?

So now a people's pride is being taken too.
Pride in self. Pride in work. Pride in country,
where much is given with no payback rules.
Why? Some people don't like waiting tables
but more than just a few who did
            grew up to own the restaurant.
My country owes me nothing.
I could not pay back what she has given me already
if I had two new lifetimes left
                        to attempt the job.

Oh the questions never answered
                    and the ones not asked.
It's as though our alphabet had never been invented,
                    but it was.
The ABC's—especially the C's
have questions that are conjured
                    by the mention of a word.
Crime. Children. Conscience. Country.
Casualty. Condominium. Cold. Crisis.
Caring. Capability. Chauvinism. Candor.
Comfort. Consumption. Control. Construction.
Chance. Cheating. Charge. Command.
Curiosity. Consequence. Charity. Cost.

Books are seldom published
when the author feels they should be
and less of those once published
                    are ever read.
I had hoped that this one
might have made the street a little sooner
then maybe someone would have been
                    incited or in touch enough
to catch a candidate and question him
                    this time out
before, without discussing issues,
he was pushed to pilot this great country
down the same old corridors and course.
Maybe next time. All of us must train ourselves
to believe there will be at least one next time.

PARADING THE COLORS

Red should not always stand for blood
not even that spilled by our fathers
          and our sons
in the great parade of wars with numbers
     one.
     two.
     three?
Red is a sunset color
a painted desert dye
the color of the Arizona plains
and at certain times, the West Virginia sky.

Pride and purity may use the color *white*.
But snow-topped Colorado mountains,
ice across the Great Lakes in December
and Alaska every day of winter time
          claimed the color first.
Not to mention that long strand of sandy Utah
and every Massachusetts/California beach.

So many uniforms are *blue*
that we forget the Truckee and the Mississippi
blue sky ocean to ocean,
        blue ocean sky to sky.
Atlantic and Pacific have always been not green
              but blue.

I know my history lesson,
                    I learned it well
that this nation to become a nation
ran forward into battle shouting *freedom!*
And often bore the tattered tri-color
                              home again
for men to mend
            and start another battle new.

I am aware
that flagmakers make new fortunes
every Veterans/Decoration Day,
and broken bodies bathed in canvas
                    and the stars and stripes
have slid off ten thousand ships
                maybe twenty thousand more,
to rest upon the bottom of the mother sea.
Excelsior at Iwo Jima.
                Bully at Bull Run.
A *step for man and mankind*
                    murmured on the moon
Peace with honor . . . somewhere.

Mothers of dead sons have pride. Me too.
But I would rather paint my colors
                on a bright balloon—
children then would wave at me
and chase my shadow.

Old men who sit at tables making wars
don't do so in my name again.
It has taken me two hundred years
to come down to this place.
I have earned the right to see *red*, *white*, and *blue*
not on a battered standard borne in battle
                but on my brother's face.

I love my flag.
To me it stands for love
kindness even to my enemy
and most of all, for brotherhood.

POSITION

I'm neither right nor left
and certainly not center.
To me to be among
the silent majority
means to be among the dead.
And for me
no two or ten or two hundred
make up a minority.
Every man is such
because every man is different.

If I met a man
who looked like me
and thought like me
and walked and spoke like me
and was no different from me
in any way,
only then would I consider slaying him
for he would have stolen from me
all those truths
and all those lies
I'd found out for myself.

All the living
that had brought me here
that man would have erased
by being just like me.

But kill a man unlike myself?
        Not likely.
There might be something
I could learn from him.

There is so much I need to know,
why there are no butterflies
in the world's backyard,
and when I find it out
I need to find a way to get them back.

Men trample beauty underfoot
like it was gravel.
These actions are confined
to no one country
but I resent it in my own.

Could it be that men join clubs
for the same reason
                they used to carry them
for security. But from what?

PREJUDICE

Prejudice is sensible.
Avoid time wasters
and the village gossip.
Give in to all the dislikes
you might harbor
for people on the inside
who would tear down any closeness
and confidence you might have built—
                    or manufactured—
for those you love
or those that you
would have love you.

Learn to hate all wars
        holy or otherwise
all those who take shelter
in hating cultures and colors
instead of individuals.

Black isn't always beautiful
but any man who finds it
        wholly ugly
should be shown
the other side of white.

The Jew who loves the gentile
should not do so out of tolerance
but only out of love—
if that love is given back.
The Polish joke only works
        told Pole to Pole.

Is it a badge of manhood
to bully and berate a man
or belly laugh at any jest
made at the cost of
                some minority
as long as you're not part of it?

Me? Some of my best friends
            are my friends.

THE CITY

---

*The American city is the best idea "that works"
to come along within our lifetimes. Our fathers
and our fathers' fathers put in place the wheel.
Our mother's zeal was inspiration for its turn.
As sons and daughters of the pilgrims and the
pioneers, it's up to us to keep it greased.*

THE CITY

one
How did we come by these heaps,
these stone monuments and forests.
Man can mold from sand
      cut from rock
         forge from steel
these monoliths clustered together
until their collective name is *city*?

What happens to us
what we go through
the joys and sorrows we amass
the confusion we pass off as evolution
the exchange of ideas
the stubbornness that softens
to embrace equality
however long it takes
is what the American city means.
But how did we come by these places?

A city is not something prayed up
and then answered by a people's God.
A city is man-given, not God-given,
brick by brick,
       shingle by shingle,
              board by board.
Man gives birth to cities
much the same as God gave birth to Man.
It comes up from the guts
        of people of conscience
listening to their conscience.
It's made as much from bowels and bile
as from brains and sorted-out bureaucracy.
As much from taste and tallying
            and tarpaper
as it's made from chance
        and taking chances.

Great cities
are the hubs and capstans
            of the nation,
they hold the countryside together.
Everything is not completely right
                in any city
as everything is not completely right
                within a life.
But you will always find those citizens
who care enough to make the city work.

The city works because
man has the need to live and work
and seek out others of his kind
to come into a clearing
            and make choices
of things to care about,
other people for his comfort
and to help him build his monuments
so that he might leave something
as if to say on his way out
        "I've been here."
                "I've come down this way."

Even if the generation up ahead
tears down the edifice
to make its own new statement
people go on building, emulating God
as though each cube of concrete
                was another Adam's rib
and every Eden needed populating
with spires and monoliths
and forty-story phallic symbols,
clustered carefully like stone forests
branches spread in all directions
highway, freeway, road and path
pointing out the other clustered creatures.

Foraging and fornicating,
jumping, running, standing still.
Solitary as the soldier with no weekend pass.
Joyful as the bridal bouquet caught by she who waited.
Clear-eyed as the woman
flashing her first business card.
Proud as every tailor who made a perfect fit
                        with only one rehearsal.
Sweet as children's faces glimpsed at random
through gobs of bubble gum and chocolate.

To make a city
you need the parts of people
their hands, their hearts, their vision
good and bad
their pull-together, push-together routine
when the work is hardest.

People first of all are masons,
that may account for their adeptness
in the dark at love,
hands that come in contact with so much surprise
caress a body knowingly, with passion
and no little pride.
They mount and ride each mound of love
as though it were a favored stallion
carefully and not with cunning.
So much heartache, joy and love
saws out a plank, nails down a board,
sets a brick in place, pours a sidewalk,
stitches up a siding, frames a pane of glass.

The milkman's coming, can't you hear?
The woman with her briefcase
              and her battle plan
                 is off to work—
heel and toe hardly touch the pavement.
And now a solitary man down the block
hurrying someplace—late, or trying to be early.

The walkers and the drivers slowly fill the street,
trucks belch blackness and somewhere underfoot
the subway buzzes, rumbles, slides into a station.
The workman with his lunchpail now takes root.
Doors are opened, blinds rush up
and lights go out at every corner.
Neon and street lamp need a rest.

And soon the horns and singing sirens.
Celebrations on the sidewalk,
jackhammers tunneling in or jacking off.

Black man, red man, white
waking up—starting to rebuild again,
regenerating what the politician
tore down the week before—
and more—trying harder this trip
this day—to make the city stand.
His fortress, his monument, his love
expressed by heart and hope and hand
the city's people's most important part.
His vision. Their vision.

We are forever changing, changing
though some changes in the city
do not come fast enough to help the helpless—
and that includes us all at one time or another.
They say it is still possible for Mrs. Thompson's son
to grow up and be the President
                    or aide thereof,
but dreams are harder realized as each day passes
only staying undisturbed in *once upon a time.*

two
I have gone through unfamiliar cities
                    in the night
always feeling I was little more than the interloper.
The man who changed his train
              at some forgotten whistle stop
                    unwanted and unnoticed.
And I have lived in cities that I never
                    came to know,
places where the gentle bells of evening rang
                    for everyone but me.
I have ached in cities feeling only half alive,
feeling smaller than I cared to,
                    feeling—nothing at all.

Night never was a shroud that closed me in.
The city evening—early or when the hour was late
always left me feeling I had traveled
across some not yet populated plain.

In my young years
my cries were more like whispers,
lately they've turned into a shout
as I lived or didn't live in cities where I felt
                                    locked out.
I have gone through
unfamiliar cities in the night
wanting to be familiar.

And some cities not known to me before
have welcomed me in such a way
that it was hard for me to leave
the limits and the confines of their arms.

Send me to a city I've not yet seen
and I'll send back to you more than postal cards.
I'll call out street names, monuments and parks
as though I were a native
                    or ran the local Lions Club.

Atlanta
growing quicker
than the concrete can be poured
so fast they had to build a city on a city.

The cluster of Los Angeles is not unlike
                    an overdone bouquet
and still it blooms, the salt air blowing in
from Santa Monica—permeating everything.

Houston threatens all of Texas,
it sprawls and crawls without the benefit
                    or time for zoning.
A herd of tractors stampedes across the desert
till soon the road to Dallas will be only
one more set of blocks to travel to.
                    Its friendliness is real.

Chicago worked on me a decade and a half
till I was ready for it.
If I had time to fall in love again
with some new place or circumstance
I'd court Chicago like a bold Lothario
with posies of so many kinds that I would need
to wake each morning early and march directly
                    to the flower market.

No city's like another.
In Los Angeles you live horizontally.
New York is vertical.
An elevator ride as endless as a star ascending.
Despite the dust and dirt of residence and storefront
one light snow or rain polishes its towers
                        till they shine as bright as Oz.
Subways like a spider web connect each borough
the way democracy fans out across the nation
interlocking it as railroads did before.

Boston with its Sunday Catholics
has as many hills as San Francisco
and as many ills and as many people working on their cure.
In each you find a kind of balance
that works toward equality—despite the headlines.
The women and the men of both are proud and strong.
If you're a native living somewhere else
you go back to San Francisco for stability
                        and sensibility
and home to Boston because the neighborhood you left
is always waiting, always there, still unchanged.

I maligned Detroit until I studied it.

Toward the end of seventy-nine
I traveled through St. Louis
and stopped in fascination
to watch a cardinal still there in the early winter
banging his head against a mirrored building.
I was puzzled till I realized that like Narcissus
he had found a love, however unattainable,
                              within his own reflection.
St. Louis has a certain tilt
as though it wants to be upended.
None but me thought it unusual
that at temperatures near zero
a cardinal was banging himself brainless out of love.

In Salt Lake City
you can lose yourself on any downtown street.
East, South, West or North North Street
                              in particular.
An address on West, East, North or South South
                        is not easier found.
Confusing? Yes. Not amusing if you're running
                              to a funeral,
or late for yet another guided tour.
But what a city—
made from salt and sweat, it has no peer.

three
I do not discount the ghetto
growing in the middle, on the edge
or circling each American town.
It is a set of broken blisters,
domino promises yet unmade, or still unkept
by all the mayors, every president
and each elected, each appointed cabinet
                              down the years.
The backyard of the White House is no cleaner
                              or kept up
than Philadelphia's inner city.
The citizens in mangers are no less citizens
than those who live in mansions on the hill,
and yet we go on buying their sympathy and silence
with food stamps and the honor roll of welfare.

Welfare.
Who coined the word?
Do you feed a family bent with hunger
and call it charity because it's given?
Being born amid the wealth and health
of this prized nation
without the chance to own your share
is to be stillborn, or still to be born.

Is it *hope* that keeps the ghetto going?
Not indolence, for some have come away.

The fanfare for the common man
was tapped out on the street
long before our Copland found it in his head
and trapped it into bars of music.

Common!
There's an adjective that sings for me.
It's orchestrated out of brass yet has more class
                             than crystal.
The man between is neither mean nor made of clay.
Unless it's common clay.
He knows the way to bend and does.
He walks tall.
While others climb the ladders and fall down
he offers strength and toughness to his country.
He is the pulse of cities yet to come,
            townships yet beginning.
He runs the race and answers questions in the contest.
And he is never there just to be contesting.
He is everywhere and most uncommon.
Because he is the common man.

four

We love our cities
as we love our countrysides.
More than providing our commodities
they give us shelter, not just a dwelling place
but the chance for us to mingle with the tribes
to crawl within the belly of these great sanctuaries
and become anonymous or synonymous
with our sisters and our brothers.

The American city dots the country
as a nesting and a resting place,
and like the migratory bird
we take advantage of its hospitality.

Hosanna in the highest
to all the forms and faces we relate to,
and may they long relate to us.

You children, you women, you men
coming naked to this land
I extend my hand to you, my arm is yours
                    without the asking.
We'll build together, skyward from the ground.
Each of us a brick, a chink, a shingle or a board
nothing less than one small part of that ongoing main.

Keep in mind that what a city should be
is not another cemetery, not more connecting caves,
                    we've been there before.
A city ought to be cathedral-like
a monument man-made, a tool to his betterment
consecrated after due deliberation
to what he believes to be his God.
Whatever that god is, be he supernatural or scientific.
God is specific—
even if He has a different voice for every man.
We owe it to ourselves, if not some God somewhere
to try to make our cities match His mountains
                    His oceans and His mountain streams.

Never let some teacher tell you
that a city is inanimate.
A city is nothing more than people,
different colors, different kinds
a hundred different thoughts inside each head.
And since our God made each of us
                              a little different,
inside each head inhabiting the city
                              lurks a different dream.

CITIZENS BAND

Honesty goes in and out of fashion with politics and policies the citizen is not aware of. But in the end, no few men change the country—it still belongs to us.

OLYMPIC GOLD

They give medals pressed in gold
               at Olympiads
for running longer,
             swimming faster,
               throwing further
than the next young woman
             or the next young man.
Medals you can wear
around your neck on ribbons
while passing past reviewing stands:
then later framed and hung upon the bedroom wall.

Athletes train the whole
of their young lifetimes
for one small moment on the track,
in the arena, pool or ring.
Somersaulting through the air
             or bouncing on a trampoline
for just a minute
our youth can go down in the record books
                  forever.

Gold keeps rising in the marketplace,
its value doubling and more.
          Maybe it's coincidental
but as an ounce of gold keeps spiraling
                    in price
the value of a human life
          goes on
            sliding
              down
                the
                  scale.

Should the world's priorities be rearranged
to fit the politics of last week
          or the next?
Should those young athletes
who gave up all their afternoons,
their weekends and their evenings—
their childhood sacrificed to training
for a chance to palm a gold or silver medal—
be awarded crackerjacks or prizes
          for sleeping late on summer mornings?

How difficult it is to want something so much,
to be prepared for it, dressed up and ready
                    then in the end be told
chance and competition have been closed.
Some have made the correlation
connecting battle fields to playing fields.
In this there is a distant link—
if you catch the culprit who blew your brother's head off
and engage him in a battle to the death
your government will send a medal in the mail.
Why not present medallions
to that young man or this young woman
who make the world better
          by bettering themselves,
even if the legend reads
Olympics Nineteen Eighty, I Stayed Home.

What was once a contest,
Man in competition with himself,
has now been turned by politicians
          into Man against Mankind.
The trouble is that old men
          legislate the wars
just as they make up the rules for sprinting.
The young are left to trip the trigger
                    in the battles
and tear their ligaments in racing.

The more the mind and then the heart
                    considers the quandary
the clearer it becomes—
The race toward Olympic Gold
            is not Man against Mankind,
it is youth against the ages and old age
so only youth should finally decide
which, if any, arenas they will march into
                    and for what reasons.

THE WAY IT WORKS

Applause on entry.
Now the house is quiet.

The moment chooses me,
demands that I perform in such a way
as to cause ignition or continued silence,
                    the choice is nearly always mine
sometimes I hesitate, or wait three seconds;
maybe six, too long. The moment goes, is gone.
I will have within that evening
a second or perhaps a third such moment
                    yet another chance.

If I miss each setup,
or hold a note unsteadily
where I should have stopped or paused—
that ovation some had come to give
                    (triggering those who didn't)
will dwindle to polite applause.

It happens.
Lack of concentration,
an eye I should have looked into
or locked upon but didn't or would not
can cause the framework of the evening
to fall forward like a house of bent unsteady cards.

But part of my profession is the taking of risks.
When I'm unprepared, I can't prepare an audience.
Why open up, why come into the ring
                    or circle the arena?
Because somebody has to go and why not me.

Stepping on the stage
is like stepping on the starter,
sometimes you have to pump a while before the engine turns.
I am sure that there are risks in the business
                    you have chosen
and ones you gladly take.

And then there is the march,
the banner hoisted high.
Whatever cause that I espouse,
                    someone in the middle aisle
or in the bottom bleacher of the crowd
                    will be offended.
But long ago I learned a truth:
and in this life but few are given,
that if those people who have followed
                    and still follow what I do
do not yet understand that one man's freedom,
one woman's hope in jeopardy, jeopardizes all of us,
then I invite them, I insist, they pack up and go home.
They'll find others they can follow
and anyway, I'm not a leader, I'm a *needer* too.

I am open as a wound
to criticism, but not guilt.
If I join the march or hoist the flag
lend my arm or name, wave the banner
                    I do so with consistency.
For every man and every woman coming down the pike
or floating through the pipeline
in search of freedom or someone just to hold the candle.

Take advantage of my position,
abuse its privilege you say?
Why the hell do you think I worked so hard
                            to get here
                    and plot so hard to stay?
If I can't give something back to a nation
                        that affords me everything
then I don't belong.

If I have to take what some may call the low road
to help a citizen reach higher ground
I'll crawl back in the gutter once again, and proudly.

In case you hadn't noticed,
                that's how it sometimes works.

UNTITLED

She watched this child
that she had carried all these days
   these days, these days
prodded, pummeled, thumped, and slapped
by the doctors and the nurses—
it did not twitch or move.

Once she thought she saw
    a stirring
but no, the baby—if that's what it was—
      didn't move.
Then one by one the masks were lowered
and she saw the bottom half of faces
in the shabby yellow room.
All of them, even her familiar doctor,
    were strangers.

As she was lifted to the rolling table
and the wheels began to move toward the hall
she tried without success
to twist her head back far enough to see
    that still unmoving lump
as though a glance from her
might cause a rumble or at least a whine.

She closed her eyes
as all the other eyes avoided hers.
She wouldn't sleep
but, dammit, she could close her eyes.

The bed was moving through the double doors
down the too-bright hall and back again
into the shared, partitioned room.

Involuntarily the mind begins to work.
Did I stumble once or early on was there a fall?
I don't remember drinking past the second month,
                                        she thought.
Was there poison in the vitamins?
Did I will that life away?

Yes, it must have been *my* fault. But how?
The corridor was noisy now.
Finally she only stared directly up toward the ceiling.
Another turn and she was being hoisted back
            into her own small bed.

She guessed there must have been
no anesthetic strong enough
to keep her out, down for the count
until the friendly doctor,
hands washed, tie in place,
could stop by later in the day
and tell her straight ahead, but gently
complete with cultivated bedside manner
that all the pain and lack of pleasure
                    had been for nothing.

She who never planned a child,
never wanted one even as it started growing,
swelling up her stomach, kicking to get loose . . .
She, who some nights prayed the growing lump
would simply go away,
                    had now been cheated.

Toward the end
those not-so-gentle kicks had been
                        dependable
the cramps and cravings a reminder
that she was God's extension
in the art of giving life.

She guessed that later in the day
when dinner came, dessert would be red Jello
                                   or a lemon sherbet.
By Friday she'd be back at work,
sorting mail, retyping letters, answering the phone . . .
I think he's stepped out for a minute,
may I ask who's calling?

And Friday she *was* working once again
and thinking—*maybe next time.*

THE TIMES
OF MAN

Man has his seasons. His own times. And while nature makes the colors change, the moons, the tides—man is more accountable for change than he might know.

THE TIMES OF MAN

one
The first campfires of April
                    fired with green wood
turn smoky in the now unknotted night.
Flicks of fire, like tracer trails
or neon flashing on a billboard
shoot through the smoke and fade.
With them go the remnants
of the worn and wilting winter.

The smoke keeps rising higher
taking on the substance of a cloud
still there when morning comes,
then finally washed away
by those first strands
                    and slanted spirals
of the early sunlight.

The dragonflies in squadron
mount their morning charge upon
the unsuspecting rose and as yet
                    unyielding yard.
Butterflies hollow into hollyhocks
and beat the hummingbirds by minutes
                    to the foxglove.

New lambs. New day. New growth
between the rocks that line the riverbank.
And far beyond the eye's horizon,
new-turned earth for newly planted hay
nibbles at the fences and the silos,
                              interrupting farms.

Soon there'll be no thought of winter left
as spring begins to lead us
through the budding of the trees to blossoms,
past the puddles made by that last snow
and onward to the village common
and finally to the very summer's edge.
The sky begins co-ordinating clouds
before the sun has fully wakened
and now the cattle's cry
                    is finally content,
different from the moans we heard
from down the field
                    all winter long.

The embryo becomes the child.
The ladder leading upward
                    to the barnloft opening
becomes a starlit stairway to the sky.
The child, now not a child at all
discovers his new nakedness—
that now erupting, bulging body
filling out like noontide.
The perfect body
in the perfect country
at the not quite perfect time.

The girls gather with the girls
and whisper softer than a hen
withholding secrets from
                    the next nest over.

The boys drift off beyond the barn
they boast and show their
                    not quite manliness
in emulation of their fathers.
They circle like the Indians
and then perform a circle jerk.

Now all are skinny dippers
                    at the pond
all gooseflesh and a-giggle.

Man stretches, sighs or merely yawns.
Coffee by the campfire
along the roadside in the hashhouse
or poured at home by loving hands
while he pores over morning papers.
His buttocks fit in every chair,
on each abandoned anthill
or upon the coldest rock
now warming to his body heat.
Absentmindedly
he scratches at his shoulder
                    or his groin,
massages his wide shoulders,
and then goes to where men go
                        in morning.
Somewhere. Anywhere. Nowhere.

Man. The wonder of him
the thunder of his voice at whisper,
his strengths invisible till needed
his weakness magnified by want.
Imagine. His image made by God
and in His likeness.

Field mice
and the gray ground gopher
are tunneling and go traveling.
The squirrel has rummaged
through his hiding places
and now collects the long due interest
                on his meager savings.
The eagle flies, then sights a fish
swooping for the catch he misses,
then turning slowly in the air
                makes another pass.
The beaver bats the water
                and builds his beaver dam.

Spring swaggers through
                the countryside
and grass grows fresh
between the ties of unused tracks
that once linked countyseats
and cities still emerging.
The sagging fences of the railroad right of way
are covered now with wild pink roses
the way red rust has wound around
                the unused tracks.
It's hard to make a bad face during spring—
the very word erases indiscretions
and animosity to last year's foes.

Hoboing I've met men who couldn't write their names
but they told boxcar stories wild enough
to send Saroyan chasing after pad and pencil
to set down every gesture, genuflection,
                              every word.

Sowers of wheat have shrugged and said to me,
It's just a job that I do well. It's just a job.
And sounding not like Thomas Paine or Washington,
last week's politicians seeking next week's vote,
they've boasted with a farmer's eye toward the practical,
It benefits the country and what helps the country
helps my family and my neighbor down the field.
At ten o'clock, the nightly news won't put it better.

The policeman, the policeman's lot—
the havenots and the haves,
including those who haven't learned to share
are no less patriots to me
than those founding mothers/fathers
whose shoulders this, my country, was built upon
and carried down the ages.

April is the answer to the unasked question.
Will things always be and stay the same?
For better and for worse—they will not.
We know this truth to be self-evident in spring.
Bulbs bursting. Boughs bent over
tested by the weight of clustered buds,
their growing muscles to be strengthened by full blossom
and later on by pounds of pear and peach
                                    and anxious apple
through the untried summer months till fall.

Spring springs surprises faster than the wizard whizzes.
More varied than the variegated wildwood flower
are the songs she sings out to her countrymen,
and yet in terms of clocked-off time
she seems to be the smallest season of all four—
the only one to venture out upon all fours.

April won't apologize for children
seeking out new irrigation ditches
                                    and mud puddles
in their head-on search to find
the meanest place to crack and break in
this year's brand-new Easter shoes.

Sometime before the month of June last year
a black man in Chicago asked me, *What's it like
to be all over colored white?*
I sure wouldn't want to be colored white, he said.

His question went unanswered.
I guess I never thought of my own self
as being colored white or tan, opaque
                                or anything.

But it's good to be alive.
Alive right here and now.
I could have told him something. Especially that.
Though being colored any color
and thought of as just that
a black-colored gentleman or a white-colored gentleman
                a man of any outside hue
seems to filter out the proud, uneasy, troubled
                                or untroubled
man of many tie-dyed colors on the inside.
Why do people ask such questions?
And then I thought, why didn't I have
                                a proper answer?

I feel like loafing and I will.
Whose workday can I now destroy
by my own lack of interest in heading inside
while the year's first full sunshine day
                    stays outside for hours.

Come out and play, I yell
to anyone who'll listen.

The boatman or the man who works on boats
has not time to squander on the April day.
Most often you can find him caulking up his vessel
planing into shape the deck
and painting out his summer.
His woman does not wonder
what new course his sailor's soul is charting
while he feigns a sleep
or what harbor calls him next
to shape or reshape ships and boats.
She knows the sea leads out in all directions
like the wind leads out and in
and she will stay if she is told to stay.
And she will walk the widow's walk
around, around, around again
looking to the ocean, through it,
till his ship is back at port
and he's seen swaggering down the street,
                    drunk, but safely home.

Spring speaks out to each of us,
kick the guts from your old dreams
                                    she says
and start a new and better dream.
Don't waste your time on merely thinking.
Act. Do. Deliver.
Rediscover all those hidden hopes
or don't wake up yourself or others
till this time has come and gone.

Keep spring waiting at your peril.
She will not be held back
                    even by an extra storm
that wasn't in the Farmer's Almanac,
the forecast in the morning paper
or the weather watcher's caution.
Spring is the stuff of supposition
and yet its chevrons are well-earned,
an arm with hash marks to the shoulder
for centuries of regeneration.

two
Summer comes,
though not at some appointed time.
Unbridled and unheralded it jogs along
toward September in a forward,
                              headlong run.
Something prods us
from behind the curtains
and the triple-bolted door.
Those still unafraid or newly brave
now venture out to test the sunshine
at last full-powered and in full command.

The beaver blinks a moment only, then he dives.
I've yet to see the heron basking on the beach
its white wings spread in hopes of turning tan,
but everywhere the scavengers are out
in searching parties or in solitary.

The peacock preens before the peahen
                              in every season
but only man lives out the summer months
weekend to weekend, weekdays lost
so that he might strut the beach bulging, deeply bronzed
                              as his own bait
though never sure just how the trap will spring.

Where sun was once
the talisman of the young
it now confounds all ages
browning foreheads and slim bellies,
untying knots from tied-up shoulders
and strengthening the runner's leg.

And I have looked with such a longing
as the summer started counting down,
at families: mother, father
sons and daughters—together
striding from the churches
riding in aeroplanes—bunched side by side,
traveling excursion rate, row on row
or quartered to themselves.
The sons ever-vibrant,
full of father's pride,
big, robust, chests swelling
whatever age I've guessed them to be.
They were always there when needed,
conjured in the night's round middle,
true at other ends of telescopes.

The girls, the daughters, slim or round,
they all retain their mothers' calm and beauty.

Intelligence behind their eyes betrays their future
and the force they'll have upon the world
                                    as women.
Picasso or Bilitis would applaud their grace
                    the quickness of their minds.

Women are managers,
executives who call the rolls
                    and count the heads
and keep things straight and honest
with or without offices or titles
women prime the pump
and seldom get their share of water.

A woman moving lightly down the stairs
                    is fluid as a river.
Woman speaking gently or with strength
can tilt the world or make it turn
and twist and twirl across and off its axis.

The promises that lie above
a woman's inner/outer smile
could settle any disagreement,
confound Confucius and his crowd
and then come back in time to settle settlements
                            and start new worlds.
Men can only shuffle one foot
                        to the other
wondering aloud what happened
in the night or in a life of summertimes
that suddenly confused us,
changed our course and our stars.
Woman did it. Women.
Dangerous, but not destructive,
confident but never cunning,
beautiful but not once boring—
because their beauty stepped out
                            from within
and having done so
permeated each and every triumph of everyman.

Don't wonder at the distance in their eyes.
Be thankful that the distance narrows,
                    when it does.

The courage of some women has been
                    too little spoken of.
It must take special strength to lie inside
the same man's arms
for a dozen and a dozen years,
whether he be loved or unloved
                    a habit or a heartbeat.
She makes him welcome all the same.

It is man's nature to belittle women.
What a pity for ourselves.
What a heaped-up, heavy loss
that could be narrowed,
done away with to our dual advantage.
Why does misunderstanding seem to be the rule
when women and their men collide—
there seems to be no give and take.
                    Except perhaps in Spring.

And now the city child sighing
at the end of one more corn-gold summer
has lost his zest to wrench the cap
from off the fire hydrant fountain
for some measure of its wet relief.

The dog no longer moping excavates the backyard
sniffing out his early summer bone.
The horse that paced the race
then pushed ahead and won it
gets a month of pasture as reward.

Above the city on a narrow girder
with one end pinned upon a stronger piece of sky
a man who could be anyone but isn't—
better *someone* as he is,
     doffs his helmet
      shakes his head
     his shirt-off-summer ending too,
he rams another rivet into place.

The cub becomes a full-fledged scout.
And now a hill-bound eagle circles yet again,
a moment, only one—then gone.

Goodbye
to women found and those unfound.
To every kite now stretched within the limbs
of every turning-inward tree, too tall to climb.
Goodbye again goodbye.
Whoever thought the year was moving
                          from us quite so quickly.
Farewell to that young man
                    and that young man,
you hear the young girls say
as they go back to providence
                    and Providence.
Sunbleached, sunswamped, suntanned, sundown.

The beach bars now are being boarded up,
the lifeguard's back in school,
on the way to Europe first time out
or filled with brand-new confidence
                    hitching off to Hollywood
because so many glances at the beach convinced him
                          he was special.

The deer glimpsed on mid-morning outings
now come earlier or not at all.
The kittens have been weaned
and placed reluctantly in brand-new homes.

The daring young man on the flying trapeze
has once again instructed roustabouts
to hoist the net and drive the poles
                    a little deeper.
A climb. A bow. A somersault. Applause.

Goodbye, good morning and good night.

To those summer books
that grew to three
and four and then a stack
though not stacked high enough
                    to gather proper dust—
they remain unread and so unloved.
Why is it each one bears a title
taken from the Bible, Shakespeare,
                    or John Donne?
Is nothing else considered quotable
nor notable enough to bear the title
                        of last year's tome?
And last year's tome is only that.
Not nothing, but nothing more.

Farewell. I wish you more than faring well.
I know we'll meet again sooner than next summer.

three
Always in autumn the hunted hundred
moving separately from the circle
going off into the wood
                or deep within the world—

You see them just beyond the mind's edge
kneeling before the night,
                their mother church.
Taking her round face into their hands
they pull it forward
till it passes past the eye and moves
                        inside the head
there to hound the arteries, compartments
                        and canals
                within the brain.
What are they doing? Is it magic
or moonlight once absorbed then gone?
We're always left to wonder.

The ritual never varies
it is always quite the same
and once you've seen it
it remains predictable and as obvious
as the outcome of a hurried prayer
                    or a mantra done by rote.

Autumn is the mother church.
Though her acolytes have different names
                              and faces
from year to year, they never change,
nor do the mumbled chants seem different.

If there were angels in that circle
and like as not there could be
you might slowly walk the eye rim's distance
                    and catch one by the tail.
As autumn circles in on brown-tipped wings
the harvesting begins—or from a too short summer
                                    ends.
How hard the harvest is depends not on the Elements
but on the elements that make up man.

Where are the brave ones now
proud people of perception
and as near the sun could turn them
                 persons of perfection.
Remember those who came stepping
from the shadows into sunshine?
Long ago it was, before the green began.
Some trees have not a green leaf left.
No sign of living or of having lived.
Some men too are now bent over
more so than they were with fall's first double bow.

Something,
something isn't,
something isn't right.
Something like a speck of sand
                 inside an oyster
itches and has need of being scratched.

Some who ventured out in summer
are counting pumpkins now,
making pickles, stripping squash,
measuring the size of every vegetable
sorting each one out according to the price
                 its marketing should bring
as compared to what was spent in the planting
                 and the tending.

This small task done
man moves back inside himself,
withdraws even further.
With nothing but a mirror
in the mind or on the wall
man has trained himself so well,
built up his disguises
                and his forts
till even sagging muscles flex back
each time he sees his own reflection.

There between the hedge and that old oak
a fat gray squirrel sits in mid-life
unmoving but for batting eyes
that seem to circle noonlike in his head.
He isn't bored but seems to be deciding
with some degree of contemplation
                the order of things.
Should I forage for the last short grass
still alive within the neighborhood
or begin the stocking up again
of life's free acorns?

Everything that moves
does so with precision—
thrashers thrashing wheat,
mice and cats, a fat gray fox
running from the blades
                of diesel-powered harvesters
as though they fled a hurricane—and they do.

In the quiet places and at night
owls grow sleepy-eyed and prop themselves
                        against high branches.

Here comes the measurer—
a bloated concertina caterpillar
sulking as quarter inch by quarter
he surveys garden walls and wells.
His statistics when collected
will not help to make a sale,
but he'll have seen the whole
                of this whole U.S.A.
within the confines of a single garden.

The beaver now repairs his dam.
Crows argue over southern routes and clime.

The hunters sneak in silently.
Not just the strong survive
the cunning fare far better.
Still all the cunning learned,
                inherited, or practiced
will not guarantee the wild-eyed animal
freedom when the trap springs shut.
The wolf who chewed his leg off
                        limps away and dies.
The shotgun blast that left an antelope in agony
is taken up and whistled by the loon.

Man, ill-prepared
even for the loneliness of evening,
now finds himself in thought again and wondering
what kind of barricade or fence to make
against the loneliest of all his nights.

The business of autumn
is letting life lie where it falls.
The business of man is picking up
himself and every brother who falls or stumbles
                        in the yellow leaves.

For every wounded stag,
guts tumbling out of gaping man-holes
not staggering amid the wood,
three dozen huntsmen brag
about *the big one* who lumbered off
stretching out their arms
till arm's length's not enough
to show the wideness of his antlers.

With each applauding crack of thunder
the rain regenerates itself
till it's an unexpected flood or hurricane.
Not to worry.
All the shutters have been shuttered,
the cat's inside beneath the bed
and not a single door's been left ajar.
But this rain cannot be blotted out
by music or the newly lighted fire.
Not even making love will make it stop.
There's the hollow feeling
that something still outside should have been
                    taken up and carried forward
into the safety of the house or barn.

four
Winter's waiting in the wilderness.
All right, come in. I'd just as soon get used to you
                              right now as ever.
This year I resolve to wink at winter.
If the empty-pocket bluesers
in the winter doorways can wrap themselves
within the pages of the NEW YORK TIMES
and sleep you off, why not me?
Who am I to sulk and hibernate
when walks need sweeping up
and funerals need attending.

Winter is an attitude,
           ask the snowbird
(no different from the sparrow
except he chose to stay, not fly).
Winter is an ambiance,
a narrow alleyway through time,
not a signpost, but a sign.
Winter is a world remembered vaguely
till it blows in in all its brilliance
           then it's remembered well.

Winter's contribution to the lilac root
will not be known for months,
though tulip bulbs
may feel secure still frozen,
                who's to know?
The snow mole
doesn't stop and chatter
about the good or ill effect
of daylong cold and early darkness,
he only goes on tunneling in the snow.

Dare I suggest that winter too
affords each man another prize to ponder?
The prize of rising in the darkness
knowing black cannot be bought
but dressing for the auction just the same.

I have known some winters
to allot a share of joy,
not just in the carnival
or on the skating pond,
but even in December's silence
it seems to me the other parts
contributing to calendars
have too little quiet—
though winter can admittedly
                contain too much.

Old folks love to say
What you talkin' bout
when you've said nothing.
They know that silence
from friend or enemy
speaks chapter and speaks verse,
especially when there is little else to quarrel over
                    but the latest snowfall.

Careful!
Silence often argues more
than spit-out speech.
Listeners hanging on expected words
make up or envision what they cannot
                    will not ever hear.
Did you say *yes?* I never would have thought so.
Not now. Not here. Not in this winter, anyway.
There is always room for need in late December,
                    but I hadn't even hoped for love.
Even some friendships tangle and are lost
from lack of spoken sentences, in winter,
though others owe their birth to quiet.

If only each of us
was capable of taking seasons
                in their balance,
we might be moved to change our attitudes
as easily as we do our underwear,
our prejudices as quickly as our price.
Or learn to take advantage of the changes
in the weather and our circumstance
and term them only times of man
instead of feeling that these weather warps
were sent to bend and kill.

Long before I fell into a ditch
                with seasons,
tried to set down thoughts on thinking,
rules for dying gracefully and living in good grace,
began to bore you with the beaver's building,
detailed, but not in quite enough detail,
parts of conversations and a laundry list
of those who slip away and others who survive,
before I fashioned frost and worked the wind
into my own small mound of words,
I was working on some kind of ending—
                only an ending not an end.

five
We do not presume to stop the world
                    within a turn
and America, mine and yours, keeps moving too
despite us or because of us,
the dozen orbits she's involved in
go on mixing and and continue mixing us.

What a magic place to be in
what a magic time,
what a lack of mystery in the cradle
                    in the hammock, on the deathbed
as finally we learn
the power bright and shining
in each one of us
is only what's absorbed or given back
to this great country and its populace
to our America, yours and mine.

SETS OF
INSTRUCTIONS

Sometimes with one foot placed before the other while walking down a rail or pacing off a narrow fence, we start to stumble. A man could break a leg that way, and that's how Christmas toys are broken. We'd salvage much and save on doctor bills if we paused to read instructions.

TO THE CAPTAINS OF THE SHIP

You chiefs and corporals coming to the capital
elected, bought and brought into office,
I charge each of you with reading our history
how we arrived and what, as architects,
we expect to build, and as travelers,
                where we expect to go.

If you learn nothing from what has been written,
lived, enjoyed, discovered, uncovered, and destroyed,
then move over, get out of the way.
Do not presume to write new history for us
or make decisions without our help.

We elected you. Bought and paid for you.
And in some cases let you bribe your way
into positions we presumed might be useful to us.
Do not mistake your new high office
as one that confirms your own beliefs.
You were selected to represent the country.
The country does not represent
only what *you* believe it should.

We the people make up as many beliefs
                as there are different people.

Leaderless, we would be a people without unity.
But a doubtful leader or one who doesn't listen
                              or misreads us
can unify this country as never before.
We will know our common enemy,
he who betrayed us or she who betrayed us.

Having come this far
through wars of right and righteousness
and warring when the war was wrong,
we now look closer at our politicians.
Our government must govern not for glory
                              but for us.

Your job will not be easy, but it shouldn't be
because our needs grow ever-complicated
as we continue growing up.
If you've a special talent
            let it be the gift of sorting out,
discovering priorities that benefit the many,
the missing piece of a dusty jigsaw puzzle
hidden in our darkest corner
then put in place to solve another mystery.

You needn't chart the course
but you should never leave the wheel
of this great ship unattended.

Other nations and republics have revolutions too
and when the power shifts from those that we
                    befriended, propped up or propelled
our nation has a history of not insuring safety
                    or safe passage
for those we weeded from our family
unless they leave at once.

The freedom and the liberty of sister countries
should be a piece of ordinary business
that we and they can take for granted,
or we should stop pretending to befriend the neighbor.

Big Brother will not wreck the ship of state,
Big Business can but try.
Beware of what you term as democratic
until you learn the rules of conduct
                    we expect of you.
Know that you remain in government
only as long as you are needed and of use.
The love affair must work both ways.
There is no wrong side or right side
unless you start to operate outside the boundaries
                    of *our* needs
                        to fill your own.

You asked for, you demanded your position
and only you remain accountable.
All of us are with you, while you're with the country.
Each time we kneel to God
there is a prayer-like breath
that floats aloft from each of us
to keep our country and its leaders strong
to safe-keep all its citizens
to make us truly worthy of the world surrounding us.

Some citizens within our land are still cynical,
they feel the higher up the scandal
the closer some corruption comes to them.
And these are people not involved.
Not with the scandal and perhaps
            too little with the country.

Involvement from all sides propels a nation—
Democracy cannot be maintained by dreams alone.
The strength is in the deed,
the weakness in unwillingness
            to perform the deed.

If to love the country were enough
then loafers would be heads of state
and those of us who work and worry
would not have time to celebrate.

If complaining did the job
then machinists could leave early
and lifeboats could be left
                    to rust and rot,
and wells would need no prime or pump.

The country's needs are many.
They are a catalogue
of all the catalogues we've made,
and this nation needs, no it demands,
every heart and hand
                    that populates it.

TO THE LAST MAN CARRYING
THE LAST GUN

You, my brother,
don't say you kill in my name
or in the name of kind mankind.

If you swing the scythe or fire the pistol
do so in your own name,
mankind has guilt enough to shoulder.

You who send the letters
do not issue even once again,
in the name of government and justice,
numbered cards to those now leaving childhood
asking them to wait in turn to fight and die
for those things none of us
has yet been able to explain even to ourselves
let alone the children coming home from wars
not declared and never understood.

Instead
if there still be those among you
willing to commit to war,
eager to do battle for the sake of battle
let him who signs the paper in the poolroom
                    or the Pentagon
be the first to shoulder arms
and the only one to feel the bullet in his head.

War is not the rally
that provides a formula for truth.
It is a telescope whose other end
is always fixed on darkness.
The minute man walks into war
he starts into a tunnel with no end.

Resolve, promise to yourself,
that if you die for God
you will do so kneeling with a rifle
propped against your own head only.

If you commit yourself to yourself,
your brother and your country
                    as well you should,
commit yourself to life.
For living is the only means of ending wars
                              or disagreements.
The dead have lost their speech and willingness to bargain
                              with enemy or friend.

The only battle that you might perceive
is one where one day you may be called upon
                    to war on war.

Please tell the boys you send away
                              to fight my battles for me
that I have no quarrels off on foreign shores.

Send them home.

I miss their smiles on subways
and their gathering on corners
to wink at passing girls
and flirt with life as it goes
                              charging by.

I wish to see no more trees
saplings or the full grown grove
cut down and sent off to the mill
returned to me and my America as sawdust.

No man is my captain
nor would Whitman, Washington or all the Willies
                              of all the wars
let themselves be led by men of war
                              and little conscience
if they were living now.

IT WAS ALWAYS WINTER IN KOREA

It was always winter in Korea—
no matter what the time of year,
the seasons ran into each other
in one long thread without a gateway.
Snow melted into snow.
       Ice iced over ice.
And sparrows like the soldiers of both sides
didn't seem to notice
       the absence of spring
or the neglect of summer on the landscape.
Some days were colder than others,
       that's all
but even looking back through army snapshots
I come across no comrades, no buddies
posing or going about their business
       with their shirts off.
Only black and whites or slides,
but even they look faded—
black and white like winter.

One shot of me and a friend—
          whose name I can't remember—
shows us squatted, bent over at a table
in T-shirts, eating kimchee,
and that's the closest photograph
or photographic memory I own
depicting a single summer soldier.
I wasn't quite eighteen.
I had a year and some months yet to go
               till I would be called up
so I volunteered for the draft.
The government used to let you do that—
that way a man or boy-man
got his service over early
and headed home a certified reserve civilian—
a veteran, a hero, experienced, hardened,
a big shot till his severance pay
and unemployment checks ran out.

The first combat I saw was at Fort Ord,
down the coast from San Francisco.
During sixteen weeks of basic training
thirty-six men in my division were killed
                    or killed themselves.
An instructor, "funning it"
threw a live grenade at one recruit;
it blew off half his arm.
He was reprimanded, given four days' leave with pay
                    and then came back to work.
One night, jogging through the darkness on a hike,
a non-com coming in off pass
plowed into the tail end of our squadron
            in his nineteen fifty Cadillac
killing five men instantly, wounding seven more.
Few soldiers overseas could make that boast.
No board of inquiry was convened
                and no Inspector General came.
That never happened in The Flying Sixty-Third,
but he was told by the Commandant himself
that drinks and driving just don't mix
a popular slogan of the day.
We'll never know how many lives it saved.

Six weeks into basic,
long before the infiltration course
would take another nine men's lives,
Corporal Garner, I think that was his name,
got up from bed while the barracks slept
                              and hanged himself
from the rafter just above his bunk.
His deed did not disturb the quiet.
Only each man soloing
his individualistic snore
                    sliced the silence.
Stumbling out of bed, but half awake
on my way to take a piss
I bumped against his body
and set it twirling in mid-air.
                    I did not cry out or cry.
I only sat down on the footlocker
opposite this slowly—slower still—turning man
and staring straight ahead said *shit*.
I might have tried to wake the others,
but that emotion, the reaction would come later.
The noose around the deepening purple neck,
the head bent over, eyes bulging
                    ready to drop out like aggies.
The shape of him that morning still circles
                              in my mind.

He had been the mailman,
the quartermaster passing out reality
in envelopes of every color, twice a day.
Pink envelopes from pink-cheeked girls
some of us had left behind
                    blue envelopes from mothers
and envelopes with stamps embossed on them
from practical, utilitarian fathers.
It took the company commander one full week
to appoint another mailman
and then I think he only did it
to alleviate the bags of mail
                    that started stacking.
All of us wrote home about it
but of course the letters never left the post.
So much was going on,
being pushed and crammed into our heads
that most of us forgot to rewrite
                    the incident
in letters sent again
that finally reached their destinations.

Three men died of poisoning
                over a long weekend.
Another seven had their stomachs pumped.
We were never told and never knew
where the poison came from
or any other circumstance
related to this latest inconvenience.
We did know we were pieces of meat
                                expendable
to be delivered to the battle ground
after we'd been made ready
                for the sport.
And after these new deaths
whole sackfuls of Hersheys and Baby Ruths
were carried to the class or field each day.
Mess hall attendance dropped
and packages of food from home
were usually half eaten
by the newest mailman
                before he made delivery.

War is hell.
Especially in training camps.
I should have started realizing that
the first morning we fell into the street
                          to stand formation.
The barracks sergeant gave a little speech
                          just after roll call—
You mens, he said, *there are two things*
we don't allow and we don't stand for
                          in this man's army . . .
eagerly I listened on
I didn't want to break no rules.
. . . *racial and religious prejudice*, he continued
and gum in the urinals.
I suppose those are pretty useful truths
in army life or just in life.
The first we take to be self-evident.
Ah, but the second is much more practical
if you've ever had to clean
                a row of barracks' urinals.

Finally on a boat
that headed toward Japan
one day out of harbor you could see
the snow cone of Mt. Fuji,
then boxed inside a flying boxcar
for the ride from Tokyo to Pusan
someone said aloud, *I hear it's cold there.*
Memories of boot camp,
                      not yet completely gone
would soon be taken over by that cold.

I never talked to anyone about it much
or heard somebody else express it
but I know it to be fact
and far away from fiction,
it was always winter in Korea.
I wonder if the climate's
                      that way still?
Surely snow is not the normal covering
for ground where farmers work the earth
every day of every year.
Maybe it was only one long winter
made up by both sides for the war.

I've heard that steam rose up
          and covered everything like fog
in the Asian jungles of Cambodia
and the squatting forests
of North and South Vietnam
and that no matter
          what the time of year
it always seemed like summer there.
Someone else will have to write
                    of that
I only know for sure
that it was always winter in Korea.

A SET OF INSTRUCTIONS

one
Be something.
A winter fire.
Wind down the chimney
even if you have no chimney
and have not heard the sound
that such wind makes—
imagine how it sounds or is.

Be a churchmouse.
Think of the music, pomp
                    and ceremony.
You could overhear confessions
and sniffle at the vicar's robes
while he intones profoundly
            at christenings and funerals.

There may not be much cheese on hand
but should you choose your church
                        with caution
there'll be crackers most plentiful.

Be a cat, wound round itself
                    and sleeping
or safely tucked into a friendly lap,
rolling on your back and purring
or strutting off from your so-called owner
                    who has no notion
that you own yourself and are only
                    being kept by him
not for his duration but your own
or less if there is liver down the block
                    and no children.

Be a kitten—play on cue, your own.
Demand and you'll be granted
your own terms as owner
                    of the house.

Be a dog
sitting on hindquarters
on the dole for biscuits,
running to fetch sticks
smiling smugly inside
when your master says, *good dog*.
Of course you are a good dog.

Be a fish.
What a thought.
A slithering, wiggling curious fish,
bobbing to the river's surface
or scavenging for junk food
between the rocks that dot
or wall the river bottom.
For heaven's sake, if you become
a minnow or a spotted trout
choose a river that fishermen
                        have forgotten.
Be an octopus
(though it's no business of mine
if that's how you wind up.
I never have fancied octopi—
perhaps your being one
will help to cure my prejudice).
I can say with truth
that the octopus, like the worm,
the eel, and those other things
that slither, crawl, or creep
have always held a special dread for me.
But you should not be held
accountable for my tastes.
Perhaps you'll slither, crawl, or creep
with panache or style—
I wait to be convinced!

Be a bell that rings or doesn't.
Be a smile that was or wasn't.
A paper airplane. A paper kite.
A piece of paper waiting to be
                          written on or read
part of someone's diary
hidden underneath the bed,
or filed away marked *secret*.
Imagine being secret,
how important of you.
How delicious to be hidden
in a plain brown folder
stashed in a filing cabinet,
or shredded into thousands of you,
or even flushed—if you will pardon
                          the expression—
down pipes leading from a spy's
secret water closet.
That would make you a secret
                          inside a secret,
finally sailing on the water
still absorbed in secrecy
and the national security.

Be water in the first place.
Then paper, fish, boats, octopi
all manner of particles, things,
matter, objects, stuff and other stuff
wanted and unwanted
would find their way to you,
and you could sort them out.

Be a poet and maligned.

Be a shipment that's consigned.

Be a bee and pollinate.
Be a bureaucrat and legislate.

Be a chameleon maybe,
                    defying rainbows.
Be a leopard capable of changing spots.

two
A friend I know pretends to be
                    a duke.
We have enough pretenders
to thrones and other things
so don't dress up as something, be.
Old Billy knew
that *to be or not to be*
stuff and nonsense
wasn't nonsense
not in any way
but stuff to build
a wider dream on.

What is it that you want?
If you were a want ad
                    you would know
A show-off
        then you could show me.
A condominium perhaps,
a roommate, a rug, a rutabaga—
though they seldom advertise.

Do you want to be an early Edsel
(come to think of it there were no
                            later models)
A used car isn't all that bad.
It presupposes prepossession
and some kind of relationship,
like a cancelled ticket
or torn and turned-in transfers
at the second stage of trips.

Be an autograph, a single line,
why not an alphabet,
then words spoken and all those
handed down and written down,
would have to start with you.

Take care
which alphabet you choose . . .
In Japan, the books
read back to front and sideways.
Being characters in Japanese
has its advantages.
You learn another language
and you won't do
international relations
                    any harm.

Worms will argue—
there's no stopping them—
that to be alive is useless
but that's because they fraternize
with the newly dead.

Have you pondered clouds for long?
Seen how strong and near they are
yet instantly away and fragile.
Driving through them in an aeroplane
they seem like nothing,
but if you touched them
there is no doubt they would feel
like everything you ever wanted to be
            into, out of, or surrounded by.
A cloud. No single eagle
ever sat upon one
and guns while piercing some
have never killed or wounded them.
They multiply, divide
            and multiply again.
I've never seen a cloud destroyed
and certain birds are buoyed by them.

Clouds are far too gentle
to be storehouses, silos
or silver buckets made
to hold the hail or rain
                    till called for.
They may look it,
but I don't think clouds
are all that proud.

Clouds
no matter what
the schoolbooks tell you
are not conjured up
            but very real.
They glide around
like sea-bound otters
in their ocean-sky
as bright as any color wheel
                could make it.

Be something real.
A father bouncing
his first child
or scolding him with love.
A mother or a grandmama
hanging out the wash
or washing hands
before she butters bread.

When it's time, if you're a mother,
let your children go
with but one instruction
        Be Something.
There are choices
and choices that go wanting.
We wouldn't know of ghosts
but for the haunting.

three
Do not be afraid to be different,
as you should not fear being alike.

Learn that you will not be
liked by everyone you meet.
Try not to like too many things yourself,
liking everything leaves little time
for liking something *well*.

And with people
like as not
you'll like most of them.
The reason's simple.
Most people are not only
                    likeable,
but given green lights
in a world of red,
they'll love you too.

Suppose you were a prison
or a pair of chains
or even some slave ship
that thrashed the water
with oars connected
to a row of convicts—
that would not absolve you
from being good
at what you did and do.
But should you choose
the occupations listed
                    up above
I hope they give you pause
and little chance for joy.

Be a movie or a movie star
a satellite or a projector.
The last one should be preferential.
It means that you've a choice
as to what image you project,
not just something to look up to
but something to be seen
across and over, into and above.

155

Ideas have in common with the acorn
the luxury of starting small
and taking several lifetimes
to become an oak.

If you're determined
that you ought to be a pulsebeat
have a good look first
at whose pulse you'll be
metering and measuring.

You could be the nation's pulse,
a tap drum tapping
the conscience of
                    the country.

Do not contribute
to the loss
of the country's
                    language
but contribute.
That rules out being
Laundromats or *Burgerkings*.

A glass of wine, a sport,
an invention not thought up yet,
the possibilities are only limited
by the limitations you impose
on your imagination.

In the name of being
and all human beings
I ask that you begin to *be*
as soon as you begin to see
Merely being
is not quite enough.

CHOOSING NOT TO FAKE IT

March not only to your own drummer
but to your syncopation
                    and yours only
be you a band of many
or one man soloing
slicing through the silence,
the single sound heard
round the corner
or around the world.

You must set the step
or change it,
any flights of inspiration
or deviations from the printed line
should come from your head
where the pain originated.
Even an attempt to dazzle
should be thought out.

NEW YEAR'S EVE

Speak the speech I pray thee
not flippantly on the tongue.
Whatever words you have in mind
bear in mind this decade's words
have all been spoken, sung out,
and strummed from silence into sound.
The promises of men of promise have already
been broken or bent over, folded or forgotten
quicker than the ones made up in every decade
celebrated in our short but fancy history.
If you have something that needs saying
a text prepared or one now forming
                    in your hands or head
a reason for commandeering the pulpit
                              or the stage
you needn't be a sage or prophet
to be useful or of use.
Be not a soothsayer, but a truth sayer
one who slays a lie as earnestly
as a knight might skewer or carve a dragon.

Make no promises to your countryman
that you can't keep or try to keep.
On second thought, a *try* is just a poor excuse.
Come, welcome in the decade with hellos
we know the verse and chapter of each promise
made on our behalf, then broken without comment
by us—those who listen,
              by you—those who talk.

Before you risk the laughter
              of these states, united
remember that romance and rhetoric
              didn't make them great.

The arm against the wheel,
              the axle on the upswing
turns the country faster and with more
              dependability
              than the tides.
We are a document, each of us,
and we fulfill for one another
all unfilled promises made for us
even when the holder of the promissory note
              reneges.

We the people welcome leadership
as we go gladly leaderless when our
heads of state refuse or know not how
                    to bend and turn the wheel.
So speak your speech I pray you
and then get off the stage.
The Monday morning of the Eighties
has arrived as planned
and all of us who work and worry
in order that we might level off the land
                    need an early start
if that great wheel of life and love
and learning is to continue turning in its turn.

THINGS DO NOT CHANGE

Things do not change
because of accident or war.
Man is not altered,
at least not rearranged by man himself.
Man changes and is changed
                 by something else.
He evolves like the dinosaur, but slower.
Evolution is usually preoccupied
and pays no attention to proceedings
when it comes to man.
And so the wind of change
is not always accompanied by
                 the sands of time.
More often they are left behind
not even relegated to the history book.
Whatever you believe or see,
whatever horoscope you read or bible you consult—
God's own ancient diary or the one
                 you've written for yourself—
no stars, no sages, and no sayings change us.
We are altered by the alternates we stumble on.

These certain accidents
planned, unplanned, or perpetrated
that come upon us like an early fog
do make a difference.
If that fog would last or was predictable
then any change could last or be controlled.
But men have brains too small
to chronicle or keep a change
from falling backward into all the rubbish
                    that a brain contains.
Knowledge is akin to loving
the closer to reality you come
the deeper the mystery.

He who loves his country first
has time for children
and for walking,
talking in his sleep,
rolling down a hill,
and finding *one*
who supersedes all other loves.

Time will take the patriot
on an endless journey
and it will seem like overnight.
His list of pursuits can challenge
                                an abacus
and still his mind will stay uncluttered.

If you would put yourself,
                        your house in order
try thinking of your country first,
and you will learn that order
is the secret of selectivity.

Believe it. Try it, anyway.

AMERICAN SONG

The power bright and shining
held in a golden hand
the roustabout, the runabout
the tiller of the land
the rower of the boat
the ringer of the bell
the woman in the window
who waves to wish me well.

And each of those who teaches
another what is right
they make the country powerful
strong and shining bright.

The power bright and shining
passed from hand to hand
the engineer, the businessman
the child who sifts the sand
the weak who give their everything
and seem to be so strong
and she who waves as I pass by
then hurries me along.

And each of those who preaches
and each of you who might
you make my country powerful
strong and shining bright.

The power bright and shining
held in a golden hand
the lumberjack, the laborer
each woman and each man
he who fights the fires
and she who rights the wrongs
and all of those I never knew
the singers of the songs.

And each who braves the darkness
until he feels the light
you make my country powerful
strong and shining bright.

The power bright and shining
passed from hand to hand
the pilot and the soldier
and she who takes her stand
the man who writes the poetry
and he who sells the rhyme
the farmer and the family man
and she who shares my time
and those who never turned their back
on freedom and its fight
they make my country powerful
strong and shining bright.

And those who turn the wheel for me
in or out of sight
they make my country powerful
strong and shining bright.